AT THE STILL POINT

In Conversation with Saint Julian

~ Disclosures After the Revelations ~

SAINT JULIAN PRESS

Praise for *At The Still Point*

In reading these "poetic meditations" on Julian's *Revelations of Divine Love*, I found myself repeatedly having to stop—to both ponder and pray. The beauty and profundity of Starbuck's poetry reword Julian's central message: "Of how all things, No matter how small, Are held in being by the kindness of God."

~ Paul Knitter
Paul Tillich Emeritus Professor
of Theology and Religions,
Union Theological Seminary.

Ron Starbuck's lovely prayerful poems gently open us to the power of Christ's passion, the tender and transforming awakening of love's deepest purpose within each of us. In these graceful and grace-filled words, we find a balm for the broken soul, healing for the weary and wounded spirit. I found myself inspired, uplifted, and affirmed with each divine disclosure. Read this beautiful book and draw near to Christ. Pray this book and draw nearer still.

~ William B. Miller
The Gospel According to Sam
The Beer Drinker's Guide to God
The Last Howlelujah

At The Still Point

~ In Conversation with Saint Julian ~

Disclosures After the Revelations

Ron Starbuck

SAINT JULIAN PRESS
HOUSTON

Published by
SAINT JULIAN PRESS, Inc.
2053 Cortlandt, Suite 200
Houston, Texas 77008
www.saintjulianpress.org

Print ISBN-13: 978-1-955194-45-7
eBook ISBN-13: 978-1-955194-46-4
Library of Congress Control Number: 2025936755

Cover Image: *Chiesa di San Francesco a Pienza*
Photo by Ron Starbuck from Pienza, Italy

CONTENTS

A Word Uttered in Love

I was fourteen when I first encountered Thomas Merton in my clergy father's library at home. With youthful intuition, I sensed something sacred in his work—enough to know his words mattered. In *New Seeds of Contemplation*, Merton wrote: *"God utters me like a word containing a partial thought of Himself."* He explains that if we are true to this image—this thought of God we are meant to embody—we shall not be lost but find ourselves and be saved.[1]

Though I lacked a more sophisticated theological vocabulary then, something in that phrase lodged deeply within me; it reassured me that I possessed something luminous, in and with light, filled with more love than I had begun to imagine.

This was the beginning.

I continued reading—poets, mystics, theologians, seekers. I read more of Merton's work and discovered his luminous insight at the corner of Fourth and Walnut: the French mystical concept of *le point vierge—the virgin point*.[2] I learned wisdom from Zen Buddhism, D. T. Suzuki, and the writings of Sufi mysticism. I explored Joseph Campbell, not only his well-known works on myth, but also his more scholarly writings. I studied with the religious poet Vassar Miller in Houston. I kept returning to the voices that helped me understand the soul's journey: Rumi, Rilke, Jane Hirshfield, Mary Oliver, Houston Smith, Paul F. Knitter, Fr. Laurence Freeman, Martin Buber, Paul Tillich, Karl Barth, Marcus Borg, process theology, and poet-theologian T. S. Eliot.

It was in Eliot's *Four Quartets*, specifically in *Little Gidding*, that I first heard the name and voice of Julian of Norwich. His invocation of her famous assurance—*"All shall be well, and all manner of thing shall be well"*—has become a quiet refrain for me. At the time, I did not know her writings, only the resonance of those lines. Yet, something about them spoke—a note of peace that lingered. Years later, when I turned to *Revelations of Divine Love*, I found the source of Eliot's quote and a vision of Christ so radiant in mercy that it felt as if I had been waiting to hear it all my life.

Amid my reading journey, I began writing again—primarily poetry—something I had engaged in since high school and college, but now with greater intentionality. The outcome was *Wheels Turning Inward*, followed by *When Angels Are Born, There Is Something About Being an Episcopalian*, and *A Pilgrimage of Churches*. Each book represented its unique form of listening, shaped by the monastic imagination and contemplative tradition that quietly influenced me over time.

In 2011, the scope of that listening expanded. I founded Saint Julian Press—named in honor of Julian of Norwich—a woman whose voice has long been part of my spiritual landscape. A 14th-century anchoress and mystic, Julian's visions of divine love portray Christ not as a judge, but as a healer, mother, and eternal companion. Her most famous words—*"All shall be well, and all manner of thing shall be well"*—have become, for many, a quiet benediction for those enduring sorrow.

Since its founding, *Saint Julian Press* has published over seventy titles—offering a platform for poets and writers who, like Julian herself, explore the sacred, the broken, the mysterious, and the beautiful. For me, it signifies a continuation of that initial moment of listening—the word God conveys within each of us, spoken in love, echoing what Merton wrote—that *"God utters us like a word containing a partial thought of Himself."*

This book returns to Julian—not in translation, but in poetic response. You'll find poetic meditations, or *"Disclosures,"* each written in dialogue with a chapter or theme from her *Revelations of Divine Love*. My sincerest aim is to meet her where she encounters God—in longing, mercy, mystery, compassion, and love.

We live in a world still marked by suffering, yet capable of great compassion. Julian saw both clearly. She believed in a salvation that encompasses all things, lifting us from the mire of pain into the light of divine presence—not through fear, but through grace. Her visions, like those of great spiritual teachers across traditions, expand our understanding of heaven and earth. They remind us that the kingdom—or reign—of God is not only coming but is already within us.

If these verses create even a small space of peace or recognition within you, they have fulfilled their purpose. In closing, let me offer these verses written as a prayer to close this introduction and open the door to the poems that follow:

> *At the still point of creation, before what is*
> *and after what has been, time is fulfilled in the grace*
> *God gives. When we hear the voice of Christ—*
> *bear His love, and lift our hearts in Eucharistic faith—*
> *in remembrance of Him, to meet the broken body of Christ.*
> *A chalice raised in blessing, mercy shimmering,*
> *an offering to the indwelling Trinity—*
> *Father, Son, and Holy Spirit.*
> *Here, eternity bends low in benediction.*
> *Here, we are made one—with Him*
> *in a Holy Communion, an intimate*
> *union of longing and love.*
> *And all shall be well.*
> *All manner of thing shall be well.* [3]

—*Ron Starbuck*
Saint Julian Press

1. Thomas Merton, *New Seeds of Contemplation*. In one of his most beloved passages, Merton writes that God utters each of us like a word—spoken in love, bearing part of God's own thought.

2. Merton referred to it as his "Fourth and Walnut" moment—when he first realized his profound connection to every stranger passing by. He later described it as an experience of *le point vierge*, the "virgin point," where we are fully known and completely united with God.

3. These verses are original to the author–poet and serve as a contemplative epigraph, ending the introduction and preparing the reader for what follows: a disclosure.

For Julian of Norwich

May time never erase
the voice that spoke of love
when the world most needed it.
This work is offered in thanksgiving
to Saint Julian of Norwich,
who listened without fear,
and gave us a vision of Christ
where all is mercy,
and love is the meaning.

"We do not need to seek
what has already found and knows us."
—The Fourteenth Disclosure

AT THE STILL POINT

In Conversation with Saint Julian

~ Disclosures After the Revelations ~

"He said not: Thou shalt not be tempest-tossed,
thou shalt not be travailed,
thou shalt not be afflicted.
But he said: Thou shalt not be overcome."

— *Julian of Norwich, Revelations of Divine Love, Chapter 68*

THE FIRST DISCLOSURE ~ THE PASSION REVEALED
after Julian of Norwich, The Passion Visions

We may glimpse—if we are willing—
into Christ's Passion,
and in that revelation, where the Trinity
fills the heart with joy beyond sorrow—
quiet and sudden—light poured into stillness.

In the stillness of divine light,
the veil is gently lifted—
and what is revealed is Christ's suffering,
given freely in the shape of love.

There may come a time in our life
when we wonder about our place in creation—
why there is pain and suffering in the world
and whether God's mercy and love truly exist.

What gave birth to it all,
across an ever-expanding universe?

Does what we observe become true?
It is one of our oldest questions—
and a gift of God's insight.

At the beginning of all insight
there are questions we ask—
to awaken the soul.
A time to wonder and see
something of the unseen and invisible
threads and beauty of creation.
And to discover how humankind
belongs to the eternal mystery,
and is woven into it with grace.

Searching for clarity of sight—
this is where the journey begins.
This is the first insight of many
where creation's light reflects back
upon the self and soul.

Julian recounts: in the first showing
He appeared before her—
the Lord of Life, wounded and bleeding,
quiet as a lamb given over to love.

His brow was crowned with thorns of sorrow;
His face shone like a mirror of mercy;
His blood flowed outward in a red and radiant stream—
not in wrath but in mercy,
not in anger, but in love.

This grace cannot be grasped, only received.
She saw no judgment in His suffering—only promise.
No punishment—only presence, emptied and open,
drawing all the world into the stillness of compassion.

Love suffers.
And in suffering, Love saves.

He showed her that this is our beginning—
not in strength,
but in the giving away of strength.

That all shall be well not by might,
but by the fullness of divine surrender;
not by power,
but by the nearness of God,

who enters even the darkness with us,
who holds the sorrow of the world
within His own wounded hands.

She saw, too, a small thing—
round as a hazel-nut,
resting in the palm of her hand.
It was little, fragile,
as if it might fall into nothing.
But it did not.

It endures, even now—
because God made it,
because God loves it,
because God keeps it.
This was no vision of grandeur,
but of closeness.
Divine intimacy—
Of how all things,
no matter how small,
are held in being
by the kindness of God.

God is the maker of all that is made,
and in all that is made, God dwells.

In us.
In the sorrow.
In the still point where vision opens—
and we become what we behold.

Where we take in what we
are becoming in the Eucharistic Feast,

this blessed sacrament of faith,
where all shall be revealed,
where all shall be healed,

where our will seeks God,
where God's will seeks us still,
where we never cease from longing,
knowing the fullness of joy,

and our desire flows out
across all creation—
by human sight,
by an inner understanding,
by a spiritual sight indescribable,

resting in our memory of heaven.

THE SECOND DISCLOSURE ~ THE WONDER OF LOVE
after Julian of Norwich, The Visions of Love and Longing

God wills to be seen and to be sought:
to be abided by and trusted.

Here we behold the wonder of love,
the wonder of passion—
not as the world teaches, but as Heaven reveals:
a suffering so radiant it transfigures pain into glory.

Even in the darkness of our own affliction,
there is Christ's pain, not separate, but shared.
Not imposed, but offered.

Released from the source of humanity's
misperceptions, we come to see—
through our own eyes—
with bodily sight: a face upon the crucifix
shining forth, beseeching our response.

When our wisdom is sightless, when vision fails,
yet still we seek, and still we are sought—
held in an aspect of graciousness.

Love opens our belief, a flame in the hollowness
where knowing falters and sorrow deepens.

The thorn-crowned crucifix
bleeds—not drops, but rivers.
Julian saw it run as though it would never cease—
a river of grace spilling into time,
through a thousand wounds
and through one divine will.

And yet, we abide—abide in Christ,
as Christ abides in us.
Our highest desires are revealed in splendor
and mystery—not apart from suffering,
but within it. And in that gaze—
that terrible, tender gaze—
we are made whole.

WITHIN THIS VISION

There are two workings—like breath and stillness:
the soul that seeks, and the soul that beholds.
The seeking—it is given to all,
a grace within grace.

We are called to seek earnestly,
with hands unwearied, with hearts unburdened
by vain sorrow.

We are called to abide in love—
steadfast, even in silence,
even when heaven waits,
and we hear nothing at all.

We are called to trust mightily—
a full and assured faith that He
will appear suddenly, blissfully,
to all who love Him.

And so the soul learns to wait—
without murmur, to love
without ceasing, to believe
beyond its knowing.

These are the ways God wills to be seen—
in seeking, in beholding,
in becoming His own.

THE THIRD DISCLOSURE ~ ENVISIONING GOD
after Julian of Norwich, The Vision of God and Circle of Being

See! I am God: I am in all things;
I do all things; I never lift hands from my works,
nor ever shall, in worlds without end.
I lead all things to the end from without beginning,
by the same Might, Wisdom, and Love whereby I made it.
How should anything be amiss?

After this, I envisioned God as a Point—
the Mid-point of all things in heaven and earth,
the center from which all life proceeds,
the stillness within the turning.

The Divine is the Mid-point,
the point of rightness and balance,
held exquisitely, invisibly,
where creation emerges and returns.

It is the blessed point where seeing begins,
where our own perception forms the world,
and the world, seen, turns toward us—
entangled, reflected, mirrored in grace.

God is entangled with all creation,
abiding even unto the last point of time.
Let us set the point of our thought upon God,
the one who holds all within the circle.

For God moves endlessly between the Mid-point
and the circumference—the most perfect symbol—
a point equally distant from all things,
bearing an equal relationship to all.

Indivisible—Immeasurable.
Not static but ever unfolding—
here is the beginning, the radiant stillness,
the endless axis of creation.

And in this circle—without perimeter—
God is not confined, but revealed.

THE FOURTH DISCLOSURE ~ OUR CUP OF SALVATION
after Julian of Norwich, Revealing the Eucharist

> *The blood of Christ, our cup of salvation,*
> *flows unceasingly—abundant as water,*
> *eternal as love.*

In this inner vision, revealed in love
made fully known through insight given,
we are each transformed by Julian's
clarity of sight—to become our own.

We see His sweet face—
not shining now,
but pale and hollow,
a body drawn near to death.

Colorless and thirsty,
as if time itself had withdrawn.
No more flowing,
but still, and darkening.

The flesh turned
more to stone than to skin,
the beloved form
drained and discolored.

Here was the death
He did not escape—
not in vision,
not in body, not in truth.

So human,
so with us,
that even His dying
was ours.

And yet—it comes to our mind
that He has made the waters of earth
plenteous for our ease,
for love of us, to cool and cleanse and comfort.

But more than water,
He longs to give us His own Blood—
more precious, more plenteous,
most homely and near.

This is the gift He delights to give:
to wash us, not only with water,
but with love made flesh—
the Blood that binds us
to Him, to our Kind, to joy.

And still—on the altar,
a drop of water joins the wine,
disappears into its depths—
and in that vanishing, we remember

how God joined fully with our flesh,
how Christ clothed
Himself in dust—
and did not turn away.

We take into ourselves what we are becoming:
Christ, who lives in us and through us,
dwelling with tenderness and truth,
as we become His body in the world.

This is the blood He delights to give—
not in wrath, but in welcome;
not in punishment but in presence;
not to condemn but to commune.

So we drink—we partake
in this Sacrament of Faith
and become more like the One
who did not hesitate
to become like us, fully human.

THE FIFTH DISCLOSURE ~ THE ENEMY IS OVERCOME
after Julian of Norwich, Evil Overcome by Love

The Enemy is overcome by the blessed Passion
and Death of our Lord Jesus Christ.

PROLOGUE: THE WORD WITHIN THE WOUND

Before the Word was given—He let me rest in silence
to behold all that had been shown,
and all intellect within it,
as my soul could bear.

No voice. No sound.
Only thought, forming like light,
from wound to word.

And then—without lips,
without breath—
He formed in me this truth:
Herewith is the Fiend overcome.

Not shouted, but born.
Not spoken, but revealed.
This is the door to His heart.

The Word, who once took flesh,
now took my thoughts—
and made my seeing whole.

THE REVELATION

And then, He showed me a wound—
not only torn, but opened.

The side of Christ parted as a veil,
and through it light passed into my soul.

I saw His sacred heart, cloven in love,
not broken by force, but given by will.

From this wound came the river of mercy—
not in anguish, but in joy.

A joy that bore the weight of sorrow,
a bliss beyond understanding.
Not because Christ suffered, but
because He chose to suffer for love.

This is the door to His heart.
This is the wound that does not close—
because love never ceases
to pour itself out.

And I beheld in that cleft of flesh
the mystery of the Trinity—
not as doctrine but as delight.

The blood—dearworthy.
The water—washing.
The sight—sweetness.

I was pierced by what I saw,
and filled with what I could not name:
the joy of God made visible
in the stillness of a wound.

And in that wound,
I saw the Fiend within undone—
an ancient force that shames divides, and whispers:
You are not worthy of love.

But the wound spoke back:
Here, all that accuses is silenced.
Here, all that separates is mended.
Here, even you are drawn into the work of mercy.

For evil does not act alone—
it wears our faces, echoes in our silence,
feeds on what we do or fail to do.

Yet, even so, love overcomes—
not without us, but through us.

There is a veil we call evil—
but it is not substance, only shadow.
It is what covers the face of compassion,
what hides the wounds of our neighbor
behind the walls of our comfort.

Evil is not always a fiend—
Sometimes, it is forgetting
the memory of heaven
held within us—
always there, always present.
Sometimes, sin and evil are not monsters,
but our averted eyes and clouded sight,
or the turning away of the heart.
Intentional or not, it shapes our sight
and inhumanity.

But when love tears the veil,
we see again with a clearer sight.
We see what has always been true:
that the wound is still open,
and it is ours to tend.

There are seasons when
you know the fault was not outside you—
not a fiend in the dark,
but a veil in your own sight
of your making.

When you know
how thoughts can wound,
how vision, clouded,
casts sorrow across the world.

But mercy arises. And with it, love—
not abstract, not far away,
but breaking open within you,
like blood from Christ's side,
like light through a torn veil,
or through a broken vessel, begging us
to let it enter
through the cracks of our humanity,
through our too–frequent failings.

And what once seemed powerful—
fear, shame, division—
is seen for what it is:
not truth,
but confusion.

And that confusion is scorned,
not with malice,
but with laughter,
because love has given you joy
and made you new.

There is a time in our spiritual
Journey, when Christ comes unbidden
as the Incarnate Word.
Shaping the words that dwell
within us,
waiting to be spoken,
waiting to be written.

THE SIXTH DISCLOSURE ~ HEAVEN REMEMBERS
after Julian of Norwich, The Joy of Christ in Every Soul

Heaven will remember the time each one gave—
the season of their turning,
and the gift of their love.
And for that, they shall be welcomed with joy.

And then Christ said:
I thank you for what your life has given—
and especially for the beauty of your youth.
There was no voice,
yet heavenly words arose in me
surrounding my being—
it was light gathering in waves
from the farthest point of creation.
Renewing Christ's radiance within us.
And I saw the Lord
not separate and dwelling above,
but moving among us—
as a host in His own house, gathering
beloved friends for a celebration without end.
He did not take the highest place.
He gave Himself into its intimate joy.
Rejoicing in each person.
His face was radiant, and He sang
a symphony made from love alone
filling all the heavens.

Is this not our love, too, shared?
In the everyday intimate tasks
of folding laundry and linens,
in the delight of cooking
for family and friends,

in the hand that plants a garden
and tends it with a humble heart,
then helps steady the steps
of an elderly neighbor—
Christ is our joy, quietly given.

Homely. Humble. Courteous.
As a joyful servant in bearing
beyond all wonder and weight.

I saw every soul who had served Him
in any way, at any time, in thoughtfulness
was met with three gifts of glory:

First, the appreciation of Christ Himself—
as the fullness of the Trinity—
Father, Son, and Holy Spirit—
so reverent and radiant
that the soul, hearing His words,
filled to overflowing.

Second, their service
was made known
before all of heaven—
a witness to love's offering,
and the joy it brings.

And third, that the joy,
as fresh in its giving as in its receiving,
would never fade, never grow dim,
never come to an end—
everlasting upon the eternal.

And I saw,
as sweetly as it could be shown,
that each soul's time—each age,
each moment of willing love—
was held and known in heaven.

Especially the gift of youth,
offered freely to God,
answered with a joy
passing all expectations—
a remembrance and thankfulness
touched by the divine.

But even one day—
even one turning of the heart—
was gathered into glory
and met with this same love.

And the more our souls beheld
the kindness of Christ, the more we longed
to serve Him all our days,
with the full strength of our being—
without human hesitation—eternally joyful.

The Seventh Disclosure ~ Everlasting Joy
after Julian of Norwich, Chapter XV

> *God does not desire our suffering,*
> *nor dwell on the hesitations of our heart.*

There comes a time—
and we cannot say when or why—
when our souls are filled with light.

A stillness enters us
like a sovereign peace,
so bright and certain
it lifts every shadow.

There is no fear,
no sorrow,
no pain—
only the lasting joy
of being upheld by love.

But this, too, is passing.

And we are left to ourselves—
weary of the world,
worn down by our own being.
Even life itself
can seem too much to bear.

There is no comfort
except faith, hope, and love—
and these may be held in truth,
but felt only faintly.

And yet,
just as suddenly,
Christ returns the joy—
a rest so sweet and certain
that no grief, no wound,
no weight of the body
can undo it.

Then once again,
the sorrow returns.
And once again,
the hush of radiance.

Joy, then pain.
Comfort, then silence.
As if the soul were the tide.

In joy, we might say with Paul:
Nothing shall separate us
from the love of Christ.

In sorrow, we may cry with Peter:
Lord, save us—
we are perishing.

And this, too, is vision:
to know that some souls
are formed in both peace and struggle—
in brightness and shadow.

Not always because of sin,
but for the shaping
of love within us.

It is one Love—
God does not leave us,
even when we feel alone.
We are held just as securely
in sorrow as in gladness—
always, in the heart of Love.

Whether we rise or fall,
whether we feel joy
or cannot feel at all—
Christ is still with us.

God does not ask us
to remain in sorrow,
but to move through it—
and return to joy.

For bliss is everlasting,
and pain will pass away.
We are not made to follow sorrow,
but to move through it—
and rest in everlasting joy.

THE EIGHTH DISCLOSURE ~ THE DEEPER SORROW
after Julian of Norwich, Chapter XVI

The deep dying and dryness,
the hard bitter wind,
the mysterious cold—
the final suffering of Christ's Passion.

There comes a time when Christ
reveals the deeper sorrow—
not in thunder or earthquakes,
but in the stillness of death and dying—
we remember the garden—
how He prayed this cup might pass from him.
And yet, gave fully of Himself.

He does not speak.
His suffering becomes a vision
we are given outside time,
within the eternal. We see
what Julian was given to see,
And in that sacred seeing,
we are drawn into the still-certain
point of His final agony.

His sweet face—
once alive with color, fresh and ruddy,
now dry, colorless, drawn.
First pale,
then ashen,
then fading into the blue of death,
then brown and black with the cold.

This is not the glory of the Transfiguration.
This is the face of love, a loss
too profound to measure
passing from the world.

The flesh discolors, clings to bone,
the life-light slowly leaving His eyes.
Even the lips—
those lips that blessed the poor
and spoke peace over the lost—
are drained, cracked, and cold.
The warm, clean hands that healed leprosy
pale and shrunken now.

He dies slowly,
drawn out like breath caught
between heaven and earth.
And we are made to witness
what the world would
rather turn away from.

The drying of His body
was no less a miracle than the blood.
His moisture fading from within,
while wind and cold press from without—
this, too, was passion.
This, too, was giving.

The pain came not in violence alone
but in stillness:
in long abandonment,
in the deep loneliness of breath
that will not come again.

It was as if He had been seven nights
in the arms of death,
without release,
without end.

This is how He gave—
not only by the shedding of blood,
but by the slow surrender of everything
that made Him radiant to the eye.
Even beauty left Him.
Even warmth.

And still He gave.

THE EIGHTH DISCLOSURE ~ UNQUENCHED THIRST
after Julian of Norwich, Chapter XVII

The sharpest sorrow is witnessing Christ's suffering—
the One who holds all our desires and becoming.

He thirsted.
Not merely for water—
but for the union.
For all He cherished to draw near.

His voice, once rich with parables,
burst forth with a single cry.
Not for Himself alone—
but for every soul
still wandering far.

Blood flowed from Him.
His body lay empty.
His flesh, stretched and torn,
breathed only desolation.

Even the thorns
were silent now—
fixed in bone,
crowned in set stillness.

And yet, still, He held His gaze
toward the world
that wounded him,
blessing all he loved.

His thirst remained.
It was an unquenched desire.
It was God's love yearning
to be fulfilled.

And though no comfort was given,
He still gave.
Not because He lacked—
but because He loved.

THE EIGHTH DISCLOSURE ~ BIRTHING COMPASSION
after Julian of Norwich, Chapter XVIII

Christ's pain becomes our own
in which compassion is given birth.

The greater the love,
the deeper the pain.
No one loved Him more—
and no one suffered more than she did.

Mary,
whose flesh once bore His,
felt every wound
as if it were her own.

She did not stand apart from sorrow—
she was immersed in it.
Not near the Cross,
but inside the world's grief
that held Him there.

Because she loved Him most,
her sorrow exceeded all others.
The pierced feet.
The bound head,
the raw and exposed wounds.
The crown of thorns—
she endured them in silence,
as He endured them in the flesh.

This becomes His same compassion:
to be so entirely one with Christ
that His pain became her own.

And not only she.
All who loved Him
felt the fading
within themselves.

Creation, too,
faded in sorrow:
the firmament darkened,
the wind stilled,
and the earth offered no comfort.

Even those who did not know Him
were shaken.
Even those who did not believe
felt something fall away—
some unseen light withdrew from the world.

This is the love that made Him suffer.
This is the suffering
through which He opened every soul.
"Ephphathah," Christ once uttered—
to the one deaf and mute:
"Be Opened."
This is the compassion
that awaits to awaken us still.

THE EIGHTH DISCLOSURE ~ CHRIST OUR HEAVEN
after Julian of Norwich, Chapter XIX

In His pain, we see Him clearly;
knowing this, Christ becomes our Heaven.
As we come to know Christ's sacrifice,
so are we known by Heaven.

When sorrow is overwhelming,
we may wish to look away.
To lift our eyes above the pain—
toward heaven, to the light, to a distant promise.

But no distance can comfort
the soul that loves Christ.
To leave the Cross
is to leave the place of presence.

There is no heaven
apart from Him.

Not a radiant realm
or a golden rest—
but a being,
a wounded God
who chose to be with us.

You may hear a whisper—
Look elsewhere.
Turn to joy.
But our soul knows the truth:
He is our joy.

And so, like Julian, you answer:
You are my Heaven.
Not for escape,
but for union.

To remain in pain with Christ
is not despair; it is devotion.

For the one who binds us in love
will unbind us when the time comes.
We can wait.

He is our Heaven—
even in sorrow.
Even when the world withdraws its light,
Christ does not.

Let our souls speak once more,
with the clarity of love:
Christ—You are my Heaven.
And there is no other.

THE EIGHTH DISCLOSURE ~ GRACE FREELY GIVEN
after Julian of Norwich, Chapter XX

All humankind is saved—redeemed and reconciled
in Christ who carries our sin and sadness—
transformed and held
in the kindness of divine love.

He grieves for everyone
seeking salvation—and offers such
not merely our estrangements
but the sorrows we endure.

He faced not only
such separation,
but the loneliness
that came with it.

He suffered,
because He saw.
And in seeing,
He loved.

For every wound
He bore in flesh,
He bore another
in compassion.

No sorrow escaped Him.
No despair went unnoticed.

Even the sorrow
of His mother, Mary,
was carried in His pain—
as her sorrow
was born of love,
so was His.

This is how He gives Himself:
freely,
willingly,
without hesitation.

He embraced suffering
with great desire.
He welcomed it
with kindness.

He did not consider the pain
worthy of mention—
only the souls
He longed to save.

What power, what mystery
would endure thus?
What love would—
embrace such sorrow?

Only the Love that has no
beginning and no end.
Beyond time—
beyond alpha and omega.

Only Christ, whose Passion
was not taken from Him
but offered for us all
a grace still freely given now.

THE EIGHTH DISCLOSURE ~ UNCEASING WILL
after Julian of Norwich, Chapter XXI

> *Now, we are with Him in the Passion—*
> *but soon, He lifts our eyes*
> *toward an everlasting joy.*
> *He is ever near.*

We remain with Him now,
in the shadow of the Cross,
where sorrow takes form
and silence holds its breath.

Pain is not the whole story—
but it is part of it.

This is where we are:
with Christ in His dying,
bearing the ache of love
in a world still learning to see.

We may long for Him
to lift His gaze,
to smile once more,
to speak peace.

But even now—
in the stillness of suffering—
He holds us.

Not apart,
not from a distance,
but within His own pain,
as One who has chosen
to suffer with us, not merely for us.

He is our safety
even in sorrow.
He is our Heaven
even in the dark.

And when the moment arrives,
when grace has completed its quiet work,
He will turn His face toward us—
and joy will break like the dawn.

There will be no time between the last
sorrow and the first light. Only a sudden rising,
where joy breaks with the dawn—
a lifting from pain into praise.

Until then,
we are never alone.
We are never abandoned.
We are with Him in the Passion—
and He is always with us still,
and made one body with Him.
that He may dwell in us—
and we in Him.

THE NINTH DISCLOSURE ~ THE JOYFUL GIVER
after Julian of Norwich, Chapter XXII and XXIII

We each belong to Christ through the Cross—
through love made manifest within the world—
so He might receive us as joy and delight,
a gift given to Him by the Father:
His bliss, His reward, His worship, His crown.

If love had asked more,
He would have given more.
Not because it was required,
but because love will never turn away.

The Passion happened once—
but the offer never ends.
The goodness in Him
never ceases its giving.

Even now,
He would suffer again—
not out of duty,
but desire.

To create new heavens,
to raise up a new earth—
this He could do,
without labor, without grief.
But to suffer for love—
again and again,
beyond counting—
this is the highest offering
Christ could ever make.

And so He says—
sweetly and without regret:
If I might suffer more,
I would suffer more.

This is not necessity.
This is joy.
This is the bliss that cannot be measured,
for love is older than pain,
and will outlast it.
Love without beginning.
Love without end.
And in this willing passion,
Julian saw what few have ever seen:
the Trinity, in perfect love—
conceived and carried Christ's Passion.
In those three words—
Joy, Bliss, Satisfying—
she beheld three heavens,
each a window into the heart of God.

The Father rejoices,
delighting in the gift of the Son.
The Son is glorified,
crowned by the souls He has redeemed.
The Spirit is fulfilled,
resting in love's completed work.

Not one act of suffering—
but an endless delight in giving.
Not a ledger of wounds—
but an everlasting feast of communion.

No cost is counted
where love is freely received.
No price too high
for a soul who becomes His joy,
His crown,
His radiant desire.

And this is why we are an Easter people—
born not just of the Cross,
but of the unending love
that flows beyond it.

A love conceived in perfect union,
carried through sorrow,
and raised in radiant joy—
redemption, reconciliation,
and something more still.

A mystery too great to name,
yet near enough
to dwell within us.

THE TENTH DISCLOSURE ~ A PLACE OF REST
after Julian of Norwich, Chapter XXII and XXIV

In His wounded body—
as we, too, are wounded—
Christ opens a place of rest within us,
where love becomes our healing,
and longing finds its home in joy.

There is a place—
not defined by borders or stones,
but by mercy made visible
from the opened side of Christ.

A place of peace,
expansive across creation
It is not far—
but near, within the soul,
where our longing for God helps
us sense humanity as beloved.

"Lo, how I loved thee,"
He says—not in anguish,
but in luminous joy,
knowing heaven pauses to
reveal this singular truth.

He speaks—without anger,
without blame.
There is no judgment here,
only the warmth of a love
that has waited patiently
for your heart to change.

An ancient metanoia
not of coercion, but invitation.
Love invites and heals us.
It does not shame.
It welcomes.

This is the ever-present place,
created by Christ, where we belong.
He was delighted to make it so,
made in joy, and made for us.
Here, there is no judgment
but only a recognition—
we once knew, only in part;
we have always been
fully known as *beloved.*

THE ELEVENTH DISCLOSURE ~ KNOWING MARY
after Julian of Norwich, Chapter XXV

To behold Mary is to glimpse the love
that made us and holds us still.

In the Annunciation—
by saying yes to God,
she becomes the dwelling place of grace,
a sanctuary of willing love,
a soul in tune with heaven's whisper.

She teaches us to say yes to Christ,
to his compassion, to forgiveness
to healing where our naked wounds
give birth to God's love, being love-bearers.

And Christ, with joy,
invites us to see her as He does.

"Will you see her?" He asks,
as if to say: Look at who I love.
See, in her, how deeply
all are loved.

She is not far from us.
She stands beneath the Cross,
in the promise of the resurrection.
Its glory, she is joy after sorrow,
peace after pain.

There is no call to worship her,
but to see through her, to the divine
tenderness that chose her
and continues to choose us still.

She is not only the Mother of Christ,
but an image of the soul made ready—
to give birth, to bear Christ into the world.
As we must bear Christ's love.

To behold Mary
is to remember
that humility is strength,
that sorrow is not the end,
and that the love of God
is nearer than we dream.

She is our inspiration.
Yes, let it be me at this hour
of creation. To carry Christ's
future into the world.

To be present at this time
of Advent and holy waiting
fully aware of how we may help
Create the quiet spaces of the Lord.

Understanding how she is a sign
that Christ and the Trinity are
doing something new within
the world, both seen and unseen.

She is the voice of the old prophets.
Announcing that our yes to God,
to giving birth to Christ's love becomes
a spiritual surrender defying worldly empires.

And so we gaze with Christ,
not apart from Him,
but through Him.

And what He sees in her,
He sees in those He loves—
including us all.
Where *The Magnificat as Revolution*
rules the hearts of humankind
rendering a greater justice
to the poor,
the voiceless.

Earth's disempowered people
crying out.

This is the *great reversal*—
God's way
of setting right
what the world
has broken.

THE TWELFTH DISCLOSURE ~ IT IS I
after Julian of Norwich, Chapter XXVI

> *Let each soul, by God's grace*
> *through Christ's holy discernment and love,*
> *receive these words.*

We will hear it—
not in thunder,
but in stillness.
When we are *emptied*,
in a *kenosis* of faith—
a holy letting go,
in the openness of creation
where the center opens
and nothing is withheld

in the infinite possibility
of all things

when the longing grows quiet,
when the ache beneath your joy
becomes unbearable—
then, listen.

It is I,
says the voice
we have always known
and heard even in the womb.
It is I you seek
in silence and sorrow.

It is I you love
though you have not seen.
It is I who wait
within your waiting.

I am the joy
behind your joy,
the flame within
your desire.

I am the one
you serve in secret.
The one you invoke
when you do not yet know
what you long for.

Before words take on meaning
and we cannot name
the grace we are given.

We need not strive.
We need not prove.

Only receive—
as Mary received.
Say yes, as she did.
Let our souls become
the space where Christ rests.

For I am near,
closer than breath,
homely and glorified.

I am the light
you were made to see by,
the stillness that speaks
your truest name.

And your soul
will find no rest
until it rests in Me.

Let this be
our knowing:
I am that which is all.
And I am here
with you now
in this moment.

THE THIRTEENTH DISCLOSURE ~ LOVE WITHOUT BLAME
after Julian of Norwich, Chapter XXVI

> *Yes, our separation brought pain,*
> *but love was never lost.*
> *Listen—*
> *the voice of Christ rises,*
> *quiet and sure:*
> *All shall be well.*
> *And all shall be well.*
> *And every manner of thing shall be well.*

He said,
Sin is behovely.

Not desired,
but woven into the cloth
of our becoming—
not chosen,
but known.

And still,
He did not blame.

Instead,
He looked at us
with eyes
that had wept.

With hands
that had healed.

With love
that had never
been broken.

There is a place
outside the hours
where nothing is wasted.

Flowing from the rivers
of Lethe and Mnemosyne—
the deeper waters of
forgottenness and memory,
where we remember
what we have always known.

Where mercy,
like light,
touches everything—
even the wound
you thought too deep
to speak of.

This, too,
is where salvation happens—
not later,
not once you are clean,
but now.

Even before
you named the longing,
you were already
being gathered.

We learn compassion
because we have suffered.

This is what life
teaches us—
this is the
divine design.

We touch the pain
of another
because we have known
our own.

And so does He.

The Son of God
with a body like ours,
a heart that broke,
a silence He entered
and did not escape

This is not blame.
This is not wrath.
This is the mercy
that listens
before it speaks.

The fire that burns
without consuming.

The gaze
that meets
and does not turn away.

There is no waiting
for the soul to be worthy.

The well of grace
has no clock.

There is no gate,
no threshold,
no proof required—
only turning,
only the letting go
into what has always
held you.

Even time
must bow
before this mercy.

For Christ is not caught
between was and will be—
He is.
He is the beginning
and the returning end.

He is the stillness
at the center of your striving,
the silence
beneath your grief,
the yes
before you dared
to speak.

He said:
What you fear
has already been forgiven.
What you carry
I have carried.
What you regret
has not removed you
from My love.

And this—this is salvation:
not a transaction,
but transformation.
This is not earned, but given—
transforming us from within.

Not escape,
but union.

And even now,
we are not apart from it.
Love moves through us all
in the miracle of living,
in all that is miraculous
upon the earth.

We walk in the world
of clocks and calendars,
but the Reign of Heaven
has no seasons—
only the eternal cycle
of being
and becoming.

Heaven is here.
It is already within us.
It has never left.
And it cannot leave.

So rest now,
not in certainty,
but in the mercy
that does not move away.

Let our souls unfold
as they were always meant to—
without fear,
without grief,
without needing to explain.

Let love be enough.
Let this be our defiance—
to believe in joy,
when the world expects surrender,
guarding our hearts with mercy.

For it is.
And it was.
And it will be.
Always.

THE FOURTEENTH DISCLOSURE ~ CHRIST OUR MOTHER
after Julian of Norwich, Chapter XLI-XLV

Christ, who is
our kind and loving Mother,
offers mercy to feed us,
grace to restore us.
For our separation is not wrath,
but wounding—and forgetting
and love will heal us fully.

We do not need to seek
what has already
found and knows us.
The ground we stand on
is surely holy.

The prayer that rises
was planted
before our birth.
Even our longing
was a form of listening—
for the One
who has never left.

The prayer that rises
was never alone.
It began in God—
as breath becomes song.
The silence between
our asking and receiving
is not absence,
but a deeper presence.

For God is the source
of our seeking,
the ground of our longing,
the wellspring of every return.

And Christ,
our gentle Mother,
does not look away
from our wounding.

She draws near
with hands that still bear
the shape of sacrifice—
not to punish,
but to hold.

She feeds us with mercy.
She labors still
to bring us home.

And in every soul
there is a place
God has never left—
a holy dwelling,
bright and still.

Christ sits there,
not as judge,
but as light.

This is the city
of the soul.
No wrath passes through it.
Only the hush
of returning.

For even sin,
that monstrous unkindness,
is not a final word.

It is a wound
to be touched
by mercy.

A forgetting
to be met
by the memory of love.

And Christ,
our Mother,
remembers us whole.

She clothes us
in compassion.
She names us
beloved.
She does not scold,
but sings.

And the voice
is not far off—
but already
in your breath.
Every turning
was always grace,
every sorrow
already held.
You were never
lost to Love.

And this is the song:
You are mine.
You have always been.
And I am with you still—
closer than breath,
softer than sorrow,
steadfast as the womb
that once carried you
into the world
and into Me.

THE FIFTEENTH DISCLOSURE ~ RADIANCE THAT RISES
after Julian of Norwich, Chapter LXIV-LXV

Out of our brokenness
a gentle radiance rises—
brighter than a thousand suns
the soul remembering
what the world tried to forget:
that we are made for light,
and always returning to it.

Our beloved souls
never erased—
bathed in grace
and gathered so closely to Christ.

Like the bread and wine
served from his hands,
we are healed through
a Eucharistic feast
our remembrance
brought into wholeness,
into joy.

And still,
we ache to go home.

Not in despair,
but in desire—
to rest in the light
we once knew
before forgetting
taught us to fear.

We do not long for death—
but for release,
for the silence
that carries
no sorrow,
only song.

And Christ,
seeing our weariness,
does not scold,
but speaks:

"Soon—
you shall be taken from your pain,
and Christ shall be your joy."

And so the soul
rises—
not cast off,
but carried.

No longer bound
by the sorrow of flesh,
no longer caught
in the ache of separation.

It rises like a child
lifted by grace,
white as flame,
light as breath.

It does not vanish.
It is not lost.

It is remembered.
It is gathered.
It is held.

And this is not escape.
It is return.

Not the end of suffering—
but the beginning
of being made whole.

In Christ,
all that was scattered
is gathered.
All that was wounded
is healed.
All that was forgotten
is named again.

And yet—
the reign of God
is within us.

Not far, not distant,
not after death,
but here. Now.
Veiled but shining.

In God, there is no waiting.
Only fullness. We hold Him
in every moment of life.

We live between
what is broken
and what is whole.

Between the ache
of this world
and the joy
of the one to come.

We stand at the threshold—
not of doctrine,
but of the heart.

Beyond our remembrance,
something more begins:
unseen,
invisible,
yet more real
than the dust beneath our feet.

A greater reality.
A greater consciousness.
A place not invented
but remembered—
a homeland of the soul
that never forgot us.

Where we know,
and are known.
Where we are seen,
and need not hide.

Where the song of love
never ends.
And Christ—
the one who bore us,
the one who waits—
gathers us
into that joy
which has no opposite,
and no end.

BETWEEN KNOWING AND UNION

There is a moment
after the longing
but before the fulfillment—
where the soul stands quiet,
no longer asking,
not yet rejoicing.

This is the stillness
before revelation.

Where memory fades
into mystery,
and love
says nothing more
because all
has been spoken.

THE LAST DISCLOSURE ~ THE SIXTEENTH REVELATION
after Julian of Norwich, Union

Love was always our Lord's Meaning.

And at the end of all sadness
our eyes shall suddenly open
and within this clarity of sight
uncluttered by yearning
our vision fully transformed
our hope made full
our desires brought silent
in the mystery of creation

where – God as spirit
where – God as truth
where – God as wayfinder
leads us towards
our own enlightenment
and knowledge
where – Christ
as noble teacher

reveals creation's light
in this clarity, we will see
and understand—
that faith and compassion
are our radiances in
the darkness of night: the light
which is God, our everlasting day

God is the ground of our beseeching
And of our being and becoming
Love is her meaning – Love without end
and all shall be well, and all shall be well,
and all manner of thing shall be well

And this shall be the knowing:
the moment is always now—
not as clock, but as calling.
Eternally present in kairos—
In God's time.
A stillness outside our measuring
where love is never late—
everlasting.

AFTERWORD: AT THE STILL POINT
after Julian of Norwich

This collection began the way most holy things do—not with a plan, but with a listening.

Somewhere between silence and scripture, in the stillness where the soul leans inward and forward to hear what the Spirit might be whispering, I returned to Julian of Norwich. Or it would be more honest to say: Julian returned to me. Her voice, bold and clear across six centuries, did not come shouting. It came as grace often does— quietly, insistently, in the middle of the night, or in the unguarded space just before prayer.

Julian lived in a world that was unraveling. Plague, war, spiritual upheaval—it's all there. And yet, in the depths of her revelations, she heard not condemnation but compassion. Not wrath, but love. Not distance, but divine intimacy. She called Christ our Mother. She dared to speak of joy in the face of death and mercy as the most profound meaning of all things. She saw a vision of God not as a far-off sovereign but as a midwife and healer who suffers with us and draws near. One who remembers us whole.

At the Still Point is my poetic response to her Sixteen Revelations. It is neither a translation, nor an interpretation, nor a commentary. It is an echo—a contemplative unfolding of her vision in a voice shaped by my own time, my walk of faith, and my quiet astonishment at the God who still speaks.

A series of *disclosures* emerged —poems that listen as much as they speak. In Julian's theology, revelation is not an event but a relationship. God does not reveal to inform but to transform. That's why I chose *Disclosure:* each poem is both an unveiling and a confession, a prayer and a proclamation.

There are themes woven throughout: Christ as mother and companion, mercy as the memory of love, sin not as a verdict but as a wound awaiting healing. And always, the soul—your soul, my soul—as a place God has never left. Julian called it the "city of the soul," a dwelling brighter than any cathedral, where Christ sits not as judge but as light.

What held me through the writing of this book was not only Julian's clarity but also her courage. She held fast to hope in a time when hope seemed naïve. She proclaimed divine love not as a doctrine but as a lived reality, tender and absolute. And she believed that the ache we carry inside us—our longing for meaning, for healing, for return—is nothing less than the Holy Spirit praying in us, turning us back to the Source.

I don't know what brought you to this book. Perhaps it's your own season of unraveling, or maybe it's a love for the mystics. Possibly it's a desire to hear something true in a time of too much noise. Whatever the reason, I hope these poems have offered you some stillness in the turning: a hush, a pause, a place to catch your breath and remember that you are already held.

Because, in the end, this is Julian's most daring claim—that we are already found, known, and loved beyond measure. That even our searching is sacred. That God is not waiting to be discovered at the far edge of effort, but is already present in the quiet center of our being.

And Christ, everlasting and eternal, beyond the boundaries of time, sings over us, "You are mine. You have always been. And I am with you still."

ACKNOWLEDGMENTS & AUTHOR NOTES

I wish to thank friends, fellow poets, and contemplatives who offered their encouragement and insight. Their attentive hearts during the writing were an inspiration. These poems are presented in gratitude for the gift of Julian's vision—and for the living communion of those who dare to see divine love in all things.

This work is not a poetic translation or paraphrase from *The Sixteen Revelations of Divine Love* but a new collection of original poetic responses—what became the **Disclosures**. It is written in conversation with Julian's mystical insight and resonates with a contemporary contemplative path.

Rather than attempting to recreate Julian's original voice, I sought, as a poet, to rest alongside her insights—listening inwardly, writing outwardly. These poems represent a journey down the river of *Mnemosyne*, the eternal flow of memory, meditation, and becoming. They are acts of remembrance in the most reflective sense of that word—as so often used in liturgical and sacramental language.

They arise from silence—and return to silence—resting in the still point where human longing meets divine presence.

If these words offer healing, beauty, or recognition—if they awaken something within you—they have fulfilled their calling.

—Ron Starbuck
Saint Julian Press

ABOUT THE AUTHOR

RON STARBUCK is the Publisher, CEO, and Executive Editor of Saint Julian Press, a poet and writer, an Episcopalian, and the author of *There Is Something About Being An Episcopalian, When Angels Are Born, Wheels Turning Inward,* and *A Pilgrimage of Churches* four rich collections of poetry that trace a poet's mythic and spiritual journey, easily traversing the paths of many contemplative traditions. For many years, he has been deeply involved in interfaith Buddhist-Christian dialogue. He has also sustained a lifelong interest in literature, poetry, Christian mysticism, comparative literature and religion, theology, and various contemplative practice forms.

GARAMOND - Garamond
Lucida Calligraphy
PERPETUA TITLING MT – PERPETUA TITLING

www.ingramcontent.com/pod-product-compliance
Lightning Source LLC
Chambersburg PA
CBHW030500130626
46549CB00007B/2797